T0065470

God gave us a Covenant not a Compromise

DEUTERONOMY 5:3

Dr. Larry E Adams

WESTBOW
PRESS®
A DIVISION OF THOMAS NELSON
& ZONDERVAN

WestBow Press books may be ordered through booksellers or by contacting:

WestBow Press
A Division of Thomas Nelson & Zondervan
1663 Liberty Drive
Bloomington, IN 47403
www.westbowpress.com
844-714-3454

Scripture taken from the King James Version of the Bible.

ISBN: 978-1-6642-6231-7 (sc)
ISBN: 978-1-6642-6230-0 (e)

Print information available on the last page.

WestBow Press rev. date: 03/29/2022

DEDICATION

I dedicate this book to the Church of the living God and the families that struggle on the battlefield of this spiritual warfare pressing toward the mark of the high calling which is in our Lord and Savior Jesus Christ and his return.

Dr Larry Adams

CONTENTS

FOREWORD

Compromising has always been a common practice to all of us even before we became believers. It had become apart of the way we lived or was taught. There was never a question of whether we should practice compromising or not. It was considered necessary if you were going to negotiate in a situation or consider a deal with another person. It was the mutual thing to do. In this book we examine compromise for all its worth briefly. Regardless of the definition that you give it, there is a missing truth about it that we might be overlooking. Not necessarily a question of right or wrong for many of us but a cause and effect on our life. Compromising is not acceptable to people of faith even though we have good intentions. Because we are a people of faith we have only one example of how to handle situations based on our Lord and Savior Jesus Christ, With prayer and Christian principals we have no room for including another standard only the righteousness of God. God gave us a covenant not a compromise.

What people need to realize is that a lot of things we have considered to be acceptable even with the people of faith have been passed on from generations of unlearned and disobedient people who had turned their back on God. What appears to be acceptable does not make it right, for the Bible teaches us that" there is a way that seems right to a man but the end thereof are the ways of death." (Proverbs 16:25)

ACKNOWLEDGMENT

My heart and thoughts go to God in thanks for all His many blessings and gifts that have allowed me to share His word with others. I thank also my wonderful wife who supports me with unmeasurable love that reminds me to keep my eyes on Jesus. I thank my Pastor Landis Fisher for his encouragement and teaching as a dynamic man of the Gospel along with my Church family. Together we will press towards the mark of the high calling in Jesus Christ.

NO MAN CAN SERVE TWO
MASTERS; FOR EITHER HE
WILL HATE THE ONE, AND
LOVE THE OTHER; OR ELSE HE
WILL HOLD TO THE ONE AND
DESPISE THE OTHER. YE CANNOT
SERVE GOD AND MONEY.
(Matthew 6:24, KJV)

INTRODUCTION

Let me just begin by saying we learn to trust in a lot of different things for a lot of different reasons in our lives. We trust in what we see, what we know or even what we believe. As Christians once we have made that choice and have a made up mind, that type of faith should be well rooted and leaves no reason to doubt or not stand on the foundation of the one whom you have the root in. In other words the power to stand and be committed comes from the one whom you trust and have faith in that root. One standard has been accepted and satisfied. There is no room for challenge, ideas, or additions. The foundation is complete in Jesus Christ.

Therefore, the only ones who would seek another way are those whose foundation is not stable or satisfied. Compromising is what they use to challenge or change what they either don't understand or will not accept. Of course we are referring to the spiritual realities that make a different as far as understanding the purpose of uncompromising circumstances. Christians are suppose to hold fast to every word that precedes forth out of the mouth of God whether we understand it or not. Unfortunately, many Christians are weak in this area. Their interpretation of compromising seems to have another purpose involving a judgment call that overrides the word of God and perceives the situation different as to giving compromising power over the word of God as seeming to be used to keep the peace. There is no peace outside of the word of God. It may seem to be a sacrifice but is clearly disobedience to the word of God. Many Christians are so involved in situations emotionally that they are drawn into the use of compromising as they say will help bring together others. But on the other hand scripture teach us "can two walk together except they agree". (Amos 3:3)

Spiritual compromising is not for Christians because thats the way we live, spiritually. Not compromising. Spiritual compromising does not mean bringing two standards together because there is only one right and Godly way, Jesus. (John 14:6)

GUARD YOUR HEART ABOVE ALL ELSE, FOR IT DETERMINES THE COURSE OF YOUR LIFE.
(Proverbs 4:23, KJV)

WE HAVE NOTHING TO NEGOTIATE

Our Creator established a foundation in this world of how we should live. He did not negotiate this foundation but assured that it would be best to serve His purpose. He has also stated that He has chosen us in him before the foundation of the world, that we should be holy and without blame before him in love. (Ephesians 1:4, KJV) Even though He knew that we would have trials and tribulations while in the world, scripture also states that he who hath began a good work in you will perform it until the day of Jesus Christ. (Philippians 1:6, KJV) At no time in God's word has He expect us to solve any of our problems but that we would bring them to Him in faith. (1 Peter

1

5:7, KJV) He promises that he would never leave us or forsake us and that He is always in our presence.

(Matthew 28:20, KJV) Especially in making decisions about our life. We must never forget that everything that God created is important and according to His will. We can do nothing without Him.

We all are sinners by birth and in this journey of life we have a natural tendency to challenge our perceptions of life as we see it. Not realizing that God is in control and forgetting that we were created for his purpose. Until we are taught we will always be searching for answers about life. *"Why can "t I do what I want?', Why can't it be my way?* "In the beginning God has made it clear that if we would acknowledge him in all our ways He would direct our path. (Proverb 3:5,6, KJV) This reminder introduces us to a different perspective. A new question like *"do I want to do God's will?"* or *"can I do it anyway?"* Naturally, man can do nothing to please God, only willing. Because man has fallen from his holy and happy state of being and is now a sinner, all of his goodness to God is as filthy rages. (Isaiah 64:6, KJV) If your way is based on an imagination, sin rides on an imagination and is a lie and cannot be trusted. This is why God gave us a covenant not a compromise. And yet we compromise all the time with no respect to righteousness. Of course there is a way that seems right to a man but the end thereof are the ways of death. (Proverb 14:12, KJV)

ENEMY NUMBER ONE "COMPROMISING"

One of the first enemies we will encounter in faithful living is being tempted to compromise. Even though Satan would have you leave that door open in consideration that it might be a pass for peace and reconciliation, it is not according to the word of God. Compromising with the world has disastrous and deceptive consequences to God's people. Beginning with the philosophy of the world asking the question, "does it work?" should not be a reason to perceive compromising as the right way to achieve their purpose. Question should be" is it biblical and practical for faithful living". Scripture teaches us that there is a way that seems right to a man but the end thereof are the ways of death. (Prov 16:25)

FAITH MEANS WAR and we often time forget that we are in a very real spiritual warfare and things are not always going to be as they seem. Some of Gods greatest servants that are filled with love and compassion can err by allowing themselves to tolerate everything and everyone especially his own family members thus compromising the truth of God. His purpose may be to keep the peace but it won't keep God's word. The world will never see the peace of God that passes all understanding. Faithful living in this spiritual warfare must always depend on biblical standards no matter how it seems or what our perceptions are.

One of the biggest problems we have in this world is relationship. It started with our broken relationship with God the father. Now we find relationships complicated and difficult to understand. Most don't perceive or understand how to have a relationship or its purpose. The Bible itself is a book of relationships, first with God and then with each other. God's purpose for relationships has always been about "oneness". The same as His purpose for us that we might be one with the Father. (John 17:11) There cannot be a world without relationships. On the other hand, we must realize that In every area of our lives we will experience trials and tough decisions. We can even find ourselves tolerating unnecessary circumstances that require a different type of love. That is, "tough love". A love that comes with the debt but without understanding. (Rom 13:8) Satan will tempt you to the point where you can't see in the flesh what you need to see in the spirit. When it comes to relationships it is a very real spiritual warfare. Satan uses compromising to suck us into wrong relationships. Relationships that should not be natural *(What We Don't Understand About Relationship,* by Dr Larry Adams) but first spiritual according to the word.

A good example of being pulled into a compromising situation is in the case of Jehoshaphat in scripture. He gave his son in marriage probably to reunite the two kingdoms. He then accepted the hospitality of Ahab and gave his word to go into battle with him. Sometimes when we make decisions even for a good cause it is <u>still</u> compromising. And if you have the Spirit of God in you it will disturb your conscience. Jehoshaphat regretted that he had given his word, especially after a prophet of God had prophesied against Ahab's expedition. He then found himself being naively agreeing and trusting people more so than God. Had it not been for God's grace Jehoshaphat would have been killed. We can learn from the experiences of Jehoshaphat in how and why we should guard against wrong relationships and compromising. Scriptures teaches not to be unequally yoked with unbelievers. (II Cor 6:14) Its amazing how a Christian will sacrifice and rationalize being disobedient even though there will be serious consequences. If you have already made the mistake of marrying a unbeliever scripture tells us to remain married but try to live a godly life. (I Cor 7: 12-16) Even though scripture teaches "bad company corrupts good morals" (I Cor 15:33) don't be deceived to thinking that you need to compromise to form a social relationship. Remember God hates the wicked, so should we. (vs 5:5) His conscience was reminding him of his responsibility to the Lord. Love for the sake of unity that compromises cardinal truth is not biblical love.

Being truly faithful in this spiritual warfare will require that <u>total</u> commitment to the faith in God's word be trusted as the only way. Because FAITH MEANS WAR we recognize our enemies to be the world, the flesh and Satan. One thing we learned about this spiritual warfare is that we are never alone. And if we think about it we are members of the body of Christ and never sin alone. That sin affects the whole body. Likewise when we compromise isn't that also with the whole body? Be aware. We will never help sinners if we compromise our standards which is God's word. Nothing good has ever come out of compromising. Be a non compromising Christian.

Churches in our day are full of professing

Christians who think that it is OK to keep one foot in the world, and enjoy the pleasures of this world. They are saying to themselves "as long as I got Jesus" that makes it OK. The question is, are you sure you have Jesus? Paul tells us that in scriptures to examine ourselves whether we are in the faith : (II Corinthians 13:5) prove yourselves. No compromise is what the Gospel is all about. Scripture also teaches us that we cannot serve two masters either we will hate the one, and love the other: or else he will hold to the one, and despise the other. (Matthew 6:24) You are either for the Lord or against Him.

BUT IF NOT, BE IT KNOWN UNTO THEE, O KING, THAT WE WILL NOT SERVE THY GODS, NOR WORSHIP THE GOLDEN IMAGE WHICH THOU HAST SET UP.
(Daniel 3:18, KJV)

WHAT IS SPIRITUAL COMPROMISING?

We who are born again Christians have been washed in the blood of Christ and struggle to totally commit to faithful living and the standards required by our Lord and Savior Jesus Christ. Jesus says" I am the way the truth and the life no man comes to the Father but by me." John 14:6) Therefore, our life standards are based on the word of God. There is no need for new ideas, standards, false perceptions or compromising. In Christian living righteousness is what counts and encourages obedience. Spiritual Compromising is unacceptable and serves no purpose spiritually. There is only one way and that is the right way that has been established by our Lord. To compromise spiritually is to resist righteousness by creating a double standard and go against the righteousness of God. It resist the Holy Spirit from working in our lives. By not holding to the standards that we are committed to and trying to sacrifice in order to get along with others or making friends, even pleasing those for peace is not good. The scriptures teach us that obedience is better than sacrifice. (I Sam 15:22) By compromising what you know is against your belief

The problem is we as Christians find ourselves compromising our faith <u>all</u> the time in many situations thinking it is acceptable, possibly keeping the peace. It is a sacrifice that test our faith to the point where It can defeat the purpose of righteousness. Spiritual compromising falls in the category of straggling the fence and being caught between two opinions. It really has no form of stable commitment and faith. Spiritual compromising is the result of not knowing and trusting in our faith. If you feel that you have to compromise your faith and relationship with the Lord for whatever reason, you might want to **consider the kind of relationship you have with the Father. Compromising spiritually** has no place with Christians because there is only one way to righteousness. As Christians we need to realize that COMPROMISING IS ENEMY NUMBER ONE and is easily tempted to offer as a solution to a lot of problems. Our faith will always be tested and is a challenge to compromising. Scripture teaches us to earnestly contend for the faith which was once delivered unto the saints. (Jude 1:3) There is a way that seems right to a man, but the end thereof are the ways of death. (Proverb 14:12)

Remember Satan tried to get Jesus to compromise in the wilderness using scripture to justify a wrong understanding of the word of God to deceive the Lord. He is very deceptive with our perceptions. There is a way that seems right to a man but the end thereof is are the ways of death (Proverb 6:25). We need to learn how to use a spiritual perception when approached by anyone or any problem. The world's intention is to persuade you with what might seem to be the norm and no harm. But trust God and lean not unto your own understanding but in all your ways acknowledge him and he shall direct your path. (Proverb 3:6)

Subtlety is how a lot of godly people get lured into compromising with the world. The example given in scripture of how Jehoshaphat got lured in deeper and deeper from giving his son in marriage for what he thought was a good cause to reunite the two kingdoms. Besides that he accepted Ahab's hospitality and gave his word to go with him in battle. After making that decision he then decided to inquire of the Lord after which he realized that he had no choice, he had given his word to Ahab. We learn that we should first seek the Lord and his righteousness and all these things shall be added (Matthew 6:33). We generally get lured by the subtlety of the world by forming wrong relationships (II Cor 6:14). Wrong relationship like wrong marriages, wrong social relationships, wrong business relationships and wrong political relationships.

I have counseled many young ladies and young men who have fallen in love with what appears to be a real nice person who is non-Christian in hope that they will change that person or witness to that person through that relationship. They even have prayed about that relationship and believe that God has made an exception to the rule. Putting their feelings ahead of the truth they easily compromise what they know or believe that God will bring them together in Christ. Some how they are convinced that this relationship is right for them. It is not wrong to form a social relationship with unbelievers with the intentions of leading them to Christ such as Jehoshaphat accepted Ahab's hospitality. But don't be deceived, "Bad company corrupts good morals (I Cor 15:33) The fact is, core theological issues make all the difference in the world when it comes to unity and common ground (Amos 3:3) We must be very careful about political relationships. As Christians we believe that the only hope for America is the gospel. We realize that we should take a stand when it comes to issues concerning pro-life or pro-family issues even with unbelievers. But this does not mean that we are compromising. Not learning from his experience with Ahab Jehoshaphat entered into business with Ahaziah Ahab's son in building ships to go to Tarshish. Ahaziah was also another wicked king of Israel. And as the result of the venture the Lord broke all of the ships. This was his judgment (II Chronicles 20:35-37, KJV) As scripture says, "except the Lord build the house they labor in vain that build it" (Ps 127:1). As a Christian, even in a business relationship your goal is to honor God. So remember (II Cor 6:14) Compromising with the world is subtle and it ensnares us through wrong relationships.

"MAN SHALL NOT LIVE BY
BREAD ALONE BUT BY EVERY
WORD THAT PROCEEDETH OUT
OF THE MOUTH OF GOD"
(Matthew 4:4) KJV

WHAT SEEMS TO BE THE BENEFITS OF SPIRITUAL COMPROMISING?

Spiritual compromising seemingly has made quite an impact on Christians living in holding to the practice of sustaining a standard according to God's word. We have been taught that obedience is better than sacrifice (I Sam 15:22) but somehow we seem to perceive an opportunity to respond differently as if there are other considerations to explore. Speaking of those who have a strong foundation in their faith see no challenge to hold to the standard of righteousness estabished by God. To perceive that there is a reason to compromise spiritually demonstrates clearly a lack of trust and faith in their foundation. Spiritual compromising does not give us the freedom to analyze or judge a situation to be right or acceptable. Therefore, Christians should maintain their faith and trust in God and His word.

The benefits in the obedience of God's word are filled with joy and grace of God. For the scriptures teach us that we are blessed of the Lord, who daily loadeth us with benefits even the God of our salvation. (Ps 68:19) There are some Christians who are involved in situations as the result of compromising spiritually their relationship with others and later find that they regret that that relationship was not what they expected. The more they compromised spiritually the more it did not agree with their identity as a Christian. More and more spiritual compromising was expected in different areas of the relationship. Later they found themselves failing in being an example as a Christian struggling to keep the word of God. They are now expected to compromise whenever the situation calls for it. As much as they feel that they are being spiritually correct they are being unfaithfully compromised. Because as the scripture says, there is a way that seems right to a man but the end thereof are the ways of death. (Proverb 14:23) So we see that there is really no benefit compromising the spiritual truth for any purpose. As a matter of fact we as Christians must stand firm on the righteousness of God in every situation no matter what, rather it seems fair or not. What seems to be a benefit compromising spiritually is really a false perception of the whole circumstance.

The Bible teaches us that the law of the Lord is perfect (Psalms 19:7) how could that be if we were to compromise his word? And the keeping of them is great reward. (Psalms 19:11b, KJV)

NO NEED FOR COMPROMISING

When it comes to compromising what comes to mind is change or better ideas about the situation at hand. Compromising tempts those ideas to the point where it promotes change. There is not really a need for change but a perceived need because something is unacceptable. There are a lot of circumstances in Christian living that we don't understand especially when it comes to making choices and accepting those choices in faith. If you have been taught the right choices and guided to make those kinds of choices especially in obedience according to your faith there is no need for compromising. Compromising is a challenge to your faith.

God made a covenant with man not a compromise. There was always one purpose and standard. Because God is perfect and we are not, there is no need to add anything to what God requires. We must remember that we serve a holy God who is omnipotent, omniscience and omnipresence and perfect in everything that he does. And most of all, He loves us. (John 3:16) And He will supply all of our needs according to His riches in glory. (Philippians 4:19) Therefore there is no need for compromising. Compromising always requires more and is never satisfied. There is always a need to add or connect to. Righteousness on the other hand, has no need for additions or another way. No need for compromising. There is only one complete truth and way. (John 14:6) But we must have faith in that truth. Compromising is not putting others first as we might think but putting others over whats right. If you take the time to know what the truth is and have faith in that truth there will be no need for compromising. If you need to compromise it means that you are unsure and incomplete in your standards and faith.

There are times when we are tempted to compromise our core beliefs by bending our standards of integrity for a business deal or get counseling from ungodly sources to achieve success. In scripture, King Solomon experienced warnings against alliances with Egypt by the Lord. Solomon ignored God's command even though it was a small area of compromise. Later, he agreed to a treaty with Egypt that resulted in the marrying Pharaoh's daughter that lead to Solomon taking more pagan wives. When Solomon became old his wives turned away his heart after other gods. Therefore he no longer was devoted to the Lord. (I King11:4) The nation of Israel then became weaken until it was ultimately torn apart. This demonstrated that there are consequences even with the smallest compromises. We must hold fast to the word of God even when it seems like the right thing to do. (Proverb 14:12)

Even though we don't realize it compromising can become a way of life if we don't guide our lives after the word of God. We can become more aware of craftiness of Satan and traps. We must know that Jesus is the way. The truth, and the life.

(14:6, KJV) Compromising can be an attack on our obedience and steadfastness. It is not about whats right but what favors. It is about another perception or mindset that has no root. There is no truth in compromising to began with only choice. Scripture teaches us to keep my commandments, and live."(Proverb 4:4, KJV) There is life in the steadfast of God's word if we retain it in our hearts. In considering compromising Jesus says this "you are either with me or against me". (Matthew 12:30, KJV)

As Paul complains in scripture, "Oh wretched man that I am! Who shall deliver me from the body of this death?" I thank God through Jesus Christ our Lord. So, then, with the mind I myself serve the law of God but with the flesh, the law of sin. (Romans 7:24-25, KJV)

SHOULD WE ACCEPT SPIRITUAL COMPROMISING?

The question is never asked whether we should accept compromising as Christians. When it comes to whats right we simply assume that It is in our spirit to make whatever sacrifice is necessary to make the situation work regardless of whether it is right or not. Of course in many cases in prayer. It may seem logical but scripture teaches us that there is a way that seems right to a man but the end are the ways of death. (Proverbs 14:23) Compromising is one of faith biggest enemies. It will test our faith to whether it is firm. The unrighteous are not seeking whats right but what will fit into their own desires. Since we are considering compromising spiritually, what about the responsibility we have to the Spirit of God to do according to his word? In other words, Christians cannot compromise and be in the spirit at the same time. For there is only one right way. When seeking to compromise there is really nothing spiritual about it. There is no foundation to establish truth or righteousness. Only in the spirit and in obedience to God's word should we accept it. Obedience is better than sacrifice (I Sam 15: 22). In most cases, compromising would be considered a sacrifice not a sure thing. We need to trust in the word of God no matter what the cost. Because we are obligated to do whats right at all times even as children of God, every time we compromise it is a challenge to our spirit as what is expected of us as God's children. It is spiritual and should be based on truth and representative of the spirit that we have in us. Compromising may be considered an expression of godly love but not the love of God. You should never compromise righteousness.

COMMIT TO THE LORD
WHATEVER YOU DO AND YOUR
PLANS WILL SUCCEED.
(Proverbs 16:3, KJV)

HOW DO I KNOW I AM COMPROMISING SPIRITUALLY?

First of all know that we compromise everyday. Even if not purposely knowing, the cause is there. Paul says, "for the good that I would, I do not; but the evil that I would not, that I do. Now if I do that I would not, it is no more I that do it, but sin that dwelleth in me." For I delight in the law of God after the inward man; (Romans 7:19-22) Clearly stated we struggle as Christians in this spiritual warfare. In this spiritual warfare

Satan is busy working in the minds of men and their families. Often times we as Christians don't always perceive the areas of our lives that are affected by his deceitfulness in trying our faith. Our family environments can create issues that are not according to God's word and call for decisions based on our faith but because of our emotional relationships we will not allow the Holy Spirit to take prevalent in our lives. We often will allow these issues to continue even though it may define a weakness in our faith and spirit. Often times Satan will use our emotions against our faith in making decisions in our lives and our families. We may even know the word of God but weak in our trust in Gods power. Our relationships with our love ones may be threatening to the point of fear of lost of that relationship pending we somehow compromise our decision letting Satan have his way. It would seem like it was the best decision to make for the sake of preventing lost or keeping the peace. We will later find out the craftiness of Satan to destroy our families and love ones. In this world we will have trials and tribulations but we must examine ourselves daily to see whether we are in the faith. (II Corinthians 13:5) Let us not forget that Satan does his best work in individuals, families and in the Church. Using the flesh and the world as an influence as well as our minds to compromise the word of God. But trust not in a friend, put not confidence in a guide ; keep the doors of thy mouth from her that lieth in thy bosom. For the son dishonoreth the father, the daughter riseth up against her mother, the daughter-in-law against her mother-in-law; a man's enemies are the men of his own house. (Micah 7:5-6)

DOES COMPROMISING SPIRITUALLY HELP THE SITUATION?

Compromising unfortunately will always be a challenge to a commitment. Whether it be spiritual or just plain standard. The whole idea of compromising even spiritually is not necessarily supportive in a situation but to turn a situation towards a different perspective. Its not necessarily helping a situation but encouraging a different response to that situation. In some cases the idea is to bring together without standards a conclusive decision not even considering a foundation of truth. The only results expected will rely on our perspective of the situation.

In Christian living there really is no place for compromising. Jesus gave us a covenant not a compromise. It is His power, authority and word that rules. If the Father is one, the Holy Spirit is one and Jesus is one, why would there be any need for compromising? If we are one with the Father, then there can be no compromising. (John 7:11, 21) Therefore, compromising spiritually is not even possible for a child of God without giving up his relationship with the Father. (Matt 6:24) Actually there is nothing spiritual about compromising but the fact that it is motivated by a weak spirit and a unfaithful foundation. The right spirit needs no compromising.

Spiritual compromising is as real as sin in a deceptive form. It appears to be the normal thing to do and seems dependable in solving problems or keeping the peace. But make no mistake we are in spiritual warfare and the enemy would always appreciate you making and depending on your choices and not obedience in realizing that the battle is not yours. As believers just because we have the power of God on our side does not mean that we know how to manage it. We are growing in grace and in the wisdom of God as we face these decisions. Therefore realize that God did not give us a compromise but a covenant that we stand on His word no matter what. Compromising tests your faith and causes you to lean on our own understanding instead of standing firmly on the word of God. Its really all about where you stand. (Joshua 24:15, KJV)

Its amazing how when in a situation we are led to make decisions relating to our relationship to others even family instead of our relationship to God. And above <u>all</u> not even realize it is always a test of our faith. We are always in the presence of God and His expectation. This is another reason why man ought to pray all the time. This warfare is not over and we are <u>still</u> required to keep on our armor. (Ephesians 6:11, KJV) Compromisising is enemy number one and is not to be taken lightly. We are not wrestling with flesh and blood as if it would depend on you but spiritual wickedness. (Ephesians

6:12, KJV) Our perception of war cannot be compared to spiritual warfare, therefore we need to stand with the one who knows the enemy better than we do and thats Jesus Christ our Lord and Savior. Our Christian world view is critical when it comes to dealing with situations with our friends and family. It is influenced remarkably by our emotions and priorities. Also in what we would like to see done in the name of the Lord but not in His will. We need to make sure that our decisions glory God and His will and purpose rather than compromise what we don't really understand because we can't see the whole picture. As Christians our duty is to not compromise but turn it over into the hands of God in prayers.

**LET US HOLD FAST THE
PROFESSION OF OUR FAITH
WITHOUT WAVERING**
(for he is faithful that promised)
(Hebrews 10:23, KJV)

WHAT DOES THE BIBLE TEACH ABOUT COMPROMISING?

Though the Bible does not mention compromising specifically It does demonstrate the practical existent of it in scripture. During creation on the sixth day God created man in His image and gave them dominion over all that he had made. "And God said, Behold, I have given you every herb bearing seed, which is upon the face of <u>all</u> the earth, and every tree, in which is the fruit of a tree yielding seed; to you it shall be for meat. (Genesis 1:29 KJV) God was very specific in what he had given man. And after God had put man in the garden of Eden to <u>till</u> it and keep it God made a covenant with man not a compromise.

The Lord God commanded the man that of every tree of the garden he may freely eat; but of the tree of the knowledge of good and evil, he shall not eat; "for the day that thou eateth thereof thou shall surely die." (Gen 2:17) Obviously God had described the tree as not a tree with fruit yielding seed but a tree of the knowledge of good and evil. Man knew the difference, nevertheless he compromised the commandment of God for whatever speculative reasons. Even though temptation and persuasion played a part man was not fooled or beguiled. He had compromised the commandment of God. <u>Adam</u> was guilty of voluntary transgression against God's command. In other words a dishonorable and shameful concession. He sinned against God. Compromising the spiritual principals of God is a very dangerous decision. Adam listened to his wife instead of the command of God. (Gen 3:17)

In scripture Dinah, the daughter of Leah, whom she bore unto Jacob, went out to see the daughters of the land only to find She'chem the son of Hamor the Hivite, prince of the country. He saw her and took her and defiled her. He then fell in love with her and wanted her to be his wife and tried to compromise with the family thinking that would cover for his wrong doing. (Gen 34:!-31) Compromising does not make righteousness or cover that which has been violated. Only God can wipe away sin. It cannot be compromised or covered up. The Bible clearly teaches in spiritual examples of Christian principals that cannot be compromised. You cannot hide your motives from God He knows all and sees all.

To compromise is to make concessions or specific accommodations for another person who does not agree with a prevalent set of standards or rules. God does not condone compromising. (Psalms 119:1-4) Those who are wholeheartedly devoted in their relationship to him see no desire to compromise. We as Christians don't compromise or deviate from his standards but "walk only in his path". We hear only God's voice.

(I Kings18:21, John 8: 47, John 10:27) and

we do not yield to or permit any deviation from his word. (Deuteronomy 4:2, Psalms 119:128, Revelation 22:18-19). Regardless of the worlds concession to godlessness we should never compromise. (Joshua 24:15, Psalms 119:10, Psalms 119:15).

We should not allow anyone through deceptive philosophy that is a part of human traditions and basic principles of this world to persuade us to compromise. (Colossians 2:8, Hebrew 3:12) I Peter 3:15 says we are to be prepared to give an answer or defend the reason of the hope that is in you. We must defend the word and correct those who are in opposition (II Timothy 2:24-26) that those outside of Christ may come to their reasoning and flee from the snare of the devil. We should not compromise our biblical belief by living like the world. (Acts 20:30, I John 2:16-19). These are those who hear the word, but the interest of the world and the riches and desires for other things enter their minds and push aside the word and they become unfruitful. (Mark 4: 18-19) Jesus chastised people who rationalized their motive and questionable behavior. (John 5:4144) This is to allow this world to take precedence over Christ. (Matthew 6:24)

How do we Compromise the word?

1. When we fail to accept the word of God (**II** Timothy 4: 3-4)
2. When we place our desires, and that of others ahead of the word of God: (Acts 5:4)
3. We must accept God's word as absolute (II Timothy 3:16)
4. We must be fully obedient of his word. (John 14:15, I John 5:3, **II** John 1:6)
5. His word should not be compromised for any reason or for anyone. (Deuteronomy 17:11, Proverb 24:7, Revelation 3:15)

HE TAUGHT ME ALSO, AND SAID
UNTO ME, LET THINE HEART
RETAIN MY WORDS; KEEP MY
COMMANDMENTS, AND LIVE.
(Proverbs 4:4, KJV)

WHAT ABOUT OUR PERCEPTIONS IN COMPROMISING?

Compromising depends upon our perceptions and how we are seeing the situation. Whether we are perceiving from a selfish view or from a view choice of righteousness will make all the difference whether we will compromise or not. On the other hand, its not what you look at but how we see it. Perceptions play a big part in how we react to any situation. Compromising may seem to be necessary because we cannot see the whole picture or understand the cause and effect of a situation. Only God knows and understands the problem we face and for what purpose we face them. God has given us prayer for this purpose to learn to trust Him and not compromise what we don't know or seems right. We as Christians have the responsibility to pray for our perceptions and our minds in the sense of our responsibility. Compromising is not for Christians but for those who are seeking a way of peace or righteousness. Jesus says "I am the way the truth and the life". (John 14:6) The Bible never teaches us to solve every problem nor be responsible for but to pray always and trust in the word of God. (Ps 118:8) We don't have a responsibility to compromise but we are responsible to pray and wait on the Lord and bring all of our burdens to the Lord. (Matthew 11:28-30) Our perceptions can be a liability if we use them to persuade others to have our way instead of the will of God. We find ourselves compromising in so many ways that we don't even realize that most times it comes from our perceptions. This is why the scripture tells us to have you this same mind that was in Christ Jesus (Philippians 2:5). The mind is the battlefield of Satan and compromising is a tool of his to persuade Christians and non believers to challenge the truth and obedience. People who feel they need to compromise have a bad sense of perception.

BEING CONFIDENT OF THIS
VERY THING, THAT HE WHO
HATH BEGUN A GOOD WORK IN
YOU WILL PERFORM IT UNTIL
THE DAY OF JESUS CHRIST;
(Philipians 1:6, KJV)

WHY SHOULD WE AVOID SPIRITUAL COMPROMISING?

Considering what we have learned about compromising spiritually, there is really nothing spiritual about compromising except it demonstrates a weakness in our spirit. We have a choice in any given situation to act responsible as a faithful person trusting in God or someone seeking another motive. Avoiding compromising can be difficult because of our perceptions. Our perceptions often changes with our understanding. This is why we must continue in Gods word to keep our visions clear and getting strenght and guidance from our understanding that will help us to avoid disobedience. We must realize and accept the fact that we will always be tempted to use something that God did not give us. God gave us a covenant not a compromise. And we are to learn to recognize the craftiness of Satan at all cause. As the scripture says, "put on the whole armor of God that you may be able to withstand in the evil day, and having done all, to stand." (Ephesians 6:13) "And above all, taking the shield of faith, with which ye shall be able to quench all the fiery darts of the wicked. (Ephesians 6:16) We must avoid compromising spiritually because It is against all that we believe and all that God forbids.

CHRISTIANS TRAPPED IN MATRIMONY

In this age of dispensation that Christianity refers to as the Church age, we are experiencing some devastating attacks on the families of the church. Not to our surprise that some of these attacks are brought upon us by ourselves. The first institution that God created was the family. This relationship was ordained by God. God created relationships for his purpose and the whole idea of a relationship was "oneness". God wanted man to be one with Him. Scripture teaches us that God created male and female and that the women was made for the man not the man for the women and they were both equal. (I Cor 11:8-9) Even though society has turned its back on God and his teachings and has denied the power of the Holy Spirit God has continued to be merciful and gracious with love everlasting that man might turn from his wicked ways. Realizing that it is the family that makes up the church and Satan is smart enough to know that to destroy the family was the place to start. Whatever persuasions, compromising, lies and turning our backs on God would simply open the door to destruction for the family. The bad decisions we make about serving the one who is protecting us is not realized until it is too late.

So many Christians have fallen up under matrimony not realizing what they have committed too. Believe it or not most people don't realize what matrimony and marriage is all about and therefore marry for many different reasons including selfish ones. The problem is, we have forgotten that God still gives husbands and wives but because of the stubbornness of our hearts to wait on him we find ourselves allowing our flesh and our perceptions the opportunity to help God out resulting in a persuasive attitude leading to a bad decision. Righteousness and unrighteousness seems to make no difference when it comes to our need or Gods purpose for our lives. God only joins together the righteous, in other words those who have a special relationship with Him spiritually. "What God has join together let no man take apart! The two have become one forever. If you have made the mistake of marrying an unbeliever, and I say mistake only because I assume that you are familiar with scripture that says "Be ye not unequally yoked with unbelievers for what fellowship hath righteousness with unrighteousness?" (II Cor 6:14) We should consider that God forgives and that He wants to save your marriage not make you miserable.

God has all power in Heaven and in Earth and Jesus has died for our sins and we believe that we have the authority to <u>fill</u> Gods purpose for our lives one of the most important things to remember as a believer is that God has all power and that power works but not against our will as a believer. God will not make a person do anything. He never has and never will. This is a vanity belief that God will make a spouse or child do what is right, not so. The only thing that stands in the way of God's power working in your marriage or relationships is your will to let the Holy Spirit do his work. The Bible tells us that the Holy Spirit will either draw you or drive you away. My concern is that Christians have given up on their marriage or have accepted the failure and making excuses for their spouses. They either wont go to Church or respect the church or their spouses. They make up excuses or offer false compromising in exchange for having their way. They even try to make it as difficult as they can to continue having their way. Blaming and throwing your mistakes at you and accusing you of not being the Christian you are trying to be. Not even feeling that they even owe you an explanation of why they should'nt worship with you. For whatever reason they don't fear God or you and your character as a Christian. What they don't realize is that they took a vow with the Lord first and then with each other. That means that your marriage consist of three persons not just two. You, your wife and Jesus. The Lord has put you together based on your vow. You are either joined in matrimony as one or by law as two. In other words you are not married to each other but to law. This also means there is no authority in your marriage. Your marriage may linger on for years as Satan works in your home under the conditions you have provided. Not enough prayer together, reading and sharing Gods word. Not applying the light of scripture and standing on the word of Gods concern about how your household should be run. Giving in to the power of Satan instead of being willing to allow the Holy Spirit to have his way no matter what the cost."As for me and my house we are going to serve the Lord". (Joshua 24:15) The Holy Spirit does not compromise with anybody. These kinds of relationships will hinder the Church for scripture states if a man know not how to rule his own home, how shall he take care of the Church of God". (I Timothy 3:5)

Jesus states "for I have come to set variance against his father, and the daughter against mother, and the daughter-in-law against her mother-in-law. And a man's foes <u>shall</u> be they of his own household. (Matthew 10:35-36) It all comes down to the test of faith in the home. Jesus made the sacrifice to set us free from sin whether in the home or in the world to free us from bondage but we must be willing to accept the power of the Holy Spirit.

NO MAN, HAVING PUT HIS HAND TO THE PLOUGH, AND LOOKING BACK, IS FIT FOR THE KINGDOM OF GOD.
(Luke 9:62, KJV)

CONCLUSIONS
OF CONCERN

The seriousness of compromising may not be realized at first because the perception of both parties have accepted that principal. They have not been taught or learned that there are underlying consequences resulting from the possibility of misunderstanding or dissatisfaction of the problem. We often perceive situations in the wrong way which can result in conflict with the other party. So many people have put their trust in compromising as a norm that they have become more and more blinded from the truth. There is not enough teaching about this subject as many people resist the teaching. Its unfortunate that our children are taught to compromise as way out of a problem such as lying and cheating. My concern is that we realize that we are responsible and will give an account for our motives as well as the sin of compromising righteousness. We need to reconsider our life principles and how we perceive what is acceptable to God. God loves us and there is no need to compromise even out of fear. (Hebrew 13:6)

SCRIPTURE REFERENCES

John 14:6

Amos 3:3

Philippians 1:6

I Samuel 15:22

Jude1:3

Proverbs 14:12

Luke 9:62

Proverbs 16:25

John 17:11

Romans 13:8

II Corinthians 6:14

I Corinthians 7:12-16

I Corinthians 15:33

Psalms 5:5

II Corinthians 13:5

Matthew 6:24

Luke 9:23

John 17:16

Matthew 16:24

Luke 14:28

John **14:6**

Luke 9:62

Hebrews 10:23

I Samuel 15:22

Psalms 68:19

Proverbs 14:23

Psalms 19:7

John 3:16

Psalms 19:1 lb

Philippians 4:19

Matthew 4:4

Proverbs 16:3

John 7:11,21

Matthew 6:24

Romans 7:19-22

II Corinthians 13:5

Micah 7:5-6

Proverbs 4:23

Genesis 1:29

Genesis 2:17

Genesis 3:17

Genesis 34:1-31

Psalms 118:8

Matthew 11:28-30

Philippians 2:5

BIBLIOGRAPHY OF HELPFUL RESOURCES

Bibles

1. The New SCOFIELD Reference Bible
   C. I. Scofield, D. D. Oxford University
   Press, Inc. 1967 KJV
2. The Nelson Study Bible
   Thomas Nelson Inc 1997, Nashville
   TN NKJV

Bible Commentaries

1. Understanding Christian Theology
   Charles R. Swindon and Roy B. Zuck,
   2003 Thomas Nelson
   Publishers, Nashville, TN

Helpful Biblical Resource Tools

1. Teach them Diligently
   Lou Priolo, Timex Texts, Woodruff SC.
   2000
2. The Relationship Principles of Jesus
   Tom Holladay, 2008, Zondervan Grand
   Rapids, MI
3. Self-Confrontation A manual for In-
   Depth Biblical Discipleship John C.
   Brogen, Published by Biblical Counseling
   Foundation Inc 1991 (First- Third
   Edition)
4. Joyfully Counseling People With New
   Hearts Jay
   E. Adams, Timeless Text, Stanley, NC
   2008
5. Transformed into His Likeness
   Armand P. Tiffe, 2005, Focus
   Publishing, Benidji, MN